A HISTORY OF SEX AND MORALS IN IRELAND

First published in 2001 by
Mercier Press
5 French Church St Cork
Tel: (021) 275040; Fax: (021) 274969; e.mail: books@mercier.ie
16 Hume Street Dublin 2
Tel: (01) 661 5299; Fax: (01) 661 8583; e.mail: books@marino.ie

Trade enquiries to CMD Distribution 55A Spruce Avenue
Stillorgan Industrial Park Blackrock County Dublin
Tel: (01) 294 2556; Fax: (01) 294 2564
e.mail: cmd@columba.ie

ISBN 1 85635 351 6
10 9 8 7 6 5 4 3 2 1

Cover design by Penhouse Design
Printed in Ireland by ColourBooks Baldoyle Dublin 13

A HISTORY OF SEX AND MORALS IN IRELAND

AONGUS COLLINS

MERCIER PRESS

CONTENTS

INTRODUCTION

'From prohibitions you can tell what people normally do . . . It's a way of drawing a picture of daily life,' says a character in an Umberto Eco novel. Prohibitions on sex have oozed from Irish laws and the Irish churches since time began. Which says a lot about the daily doings of the Irish. Just how successful or sensible were the efforts to legislate for the Celtic libido is the subject of this slim volume.

Until recently, the words 'sex' and 'morals' were almost synonymous in Ireland. But most people born after the 1960s regard sex as perfectly moral. What is seen as immoral is the financial skulduggery, previously unreported and un-questioned, that a succession of political scandals has brought to light.

This book concentrates on the 'golden age', when morals were confined to the erogen-ous zones, and the distinctions between church and state were slim to the point of anorexia.

Be honest: if this book were about a few dozen ugly, middle-aged men on the fiddle, would it now be in your hands?

The Catholic Church had a vicelike grip on the morals of the Irish following the Famine of the 1840s. That grip is slipping fast, but the strength of the Church's influence led to the common perception of Ireland as a pious, conservative bastion of Rome. The historical facts are different. In fact, the Hierarchy's word was law for a period of just 150 years. Before the 1840s, and after the 1980s, the bishops and cardinals had a losing battle on their hands. 'Catholic Ireland' was a comparatively brief interlude in centuries of heathenism.

1

THE BREHON LAWS

It is a myth that Saint Patrick converted Ireland completely to Christianity. He failed to change the Celtic laws on marriage, illegitimacy, divorce and polygamy. He couldn't even persuade the Irish clergy to practise celibacy. Although they were nominally Christians, the Irish continued to live by the old laws right up to the sixteenth century.

In some ways, the ancient, heathen legislation was more liberal and compassionate than that passed by twentieth-century governments. In theory, at least. As court records haven't survived, we cannot be sure how the system worked in practice.

During the Dark Ages, even in Rome – the centre of civilisation at that time – average life expectancy was only twenty-four years Staying alive for any length of time was some achievement. The laws in force in those days took a realistic approach to life.

The early Irish had no jails, apparently. Their laws were based mainly on compensation being awarded to victims, without much thought for punishing criminals – although plaintiffs probably stabbed or slashed the defendants on an ad hoc basis.

The pre-Christian Brehon Laws favoured polygamy. The Church would later attempt to stop this practice but native lawyers rose to the challenge. They unearthed references in the Old Testament to Jewish patriarchs having more than one wife. If that was good enough for the Chosen People, it should be good enough for anyone, the lawyers argued.

The Celtic legal system classified sexual relationships under numerous categories. Classifying things was one of the early lawyers' talents; they created legal systems of vertiginous complexity. They set out several classes of marriage. Most favoured was the marriage of two equally wealthy aristocrats. By the standards of the Dark Ages, the laws governing this type of marriage were pretty decent. The wife had virtually equal rights with the husband. Not only could she own property and sign contracts independently of her husband, she could veto any contract her husband tried to sign that threatened her interests. She was referred to in law as 'wife of equal dominion'.

Ultimately, however, men were more equal than women. The laws on rape obliged a rapist to pay compensation — to the victim's husband. Adding further insult to injury, the law discriminated between different types of women on the basis of social class, and awarded smaller or larger compensation accordingly.

In an ideal marriage, the husband and wife would each bring roughly the same amount of wealth into the household. Even after they had married, they held on to their own property: there was no such thing as a joint account. This simplified matters greatly in the event of a divorce.

'No-fault' divorce was available by mutual consent. There were other grounds for dissolving a marriage. A wife could leave if her husband married a second wife or concubine. The law provided a number of incentives for the offended spouse to stay on, however. This might have been because some men married again specifically in order to acquire an heir – a vital issue in a patriarchical society.

The second wife received a 'bride-price' or wedding gift from her husband. The law obliged her to give this to the first wife, however. The first wife also remained head of the household. One legal text offers the first wife a bizarre privilege: the right to attack and injure the second spouse – but not fatally – for a period of up to three days after the wedding.

Once she had recovered from being beaten around the place, the second wife would enjoy just half the status and legal entitlements of the first, but all children had equal inheritance rights. There was no such thing as illegitimacy in Irish law; English administrations were to find this outrageous.

The early Celtic laws disapproved of one-night stands and prostitution. Indeed the prostitute's son, evocatively called 'son of the bushes', was effectively disinherited, since no one could ever be sure who his father was.

The early laws were remarkably flexible about sexual relationships once two conditions were met: the relationship had to be lasting, and it had to be recognised by the woman's kin. The law recognised even a loose arrangement where the man and woman did not live together. Instead, he visited her – but with the knowledge and approval of her people.

Some classes of women, such as rich heiresses, had the privilege of taking more than one spouse at a time. Women were not allowed to inherit property outright. A father was permitted to leave property to an only daughter, but she could not pass it on to her children. After her death, the land would revert to her father's closest male relative.

As always in Ireland, there was a loophole. The relatives in line to inherit were likely to be the woman's cousins, so she could get around the law by marrying one of them. What's more, a cousin married for this reason was often classified as a second husband or male concubine.

Grounds for divorce included mental cruelty. Derision or neglect on the part of the husband was unacceptable, as was his gossiping about the couple's sex life. For its time, this was considerate. But the law also allowed the husband to strike his wife 'to correct her'. If he inflicted a blemish on her, however, that was grounds for divorce. A 'minor blemish' entitled the wife to substantial legal compensation.

A woman was entitled to divorce a man who had grown so fat he could no longer have sex with her. Impotence and sterility were other valid grounds for a wife to leave her husband. A wife could plead that her husband had failed to 'make a woman of her'; female witnesses who examined the plaintiff would verify this claim. The law also sympathised with the wife 'whose bed is spurned, so that her husband prefers to sleep with [male] youths instead, no sufficient reason having been given.' Here again, the woman was entitled to compensation.

The early divorce laws did not provide alimony as we understand it. The principle was that each partner made off with his or her belongings. The lawyers decided that a wife who had no property of her own was entitled to be compensated for the work she had put in on the farm: they awarded her a small share of the cattle and cheese plus half the fabrics made during the marriage. On top of that, the divorced wife was entitled to a sack of corn each month from her former husband. But this arrangement was temporary: support lasted only from the time the couple split to the following May Day, when marriage contracts were signed. By then, she was expected to have acquired a new man. Woe betide the wife who, in the eyes of the law, decamped without due cause. She was virtually an outlaw, and nobody could protect or harbour her.

Abortion was illegal. A man could divorce a wife who induced or procured an abortion. (The lawyers suggested that abortions were caused by women refusing to eat.) Other grounds for divorcing a wife were her being in league with the husband's enemies or bringing shame upon him.

2

CELIBACY: ROUND ONE

The man of God understood that he had
been sent not to men, but to beasts.
Never before had he known the like, in
whatever depth of barbarism: never before
had he found men so shameless in their
morals . . . They were Christians in
name; in fact they were pagans . . . They
did not enter on lawful marriage . . . They
made no confessions . . . In the churches
was heard neither the voice of a preacher
nor of a singer.

That was how Saint Bernard described the Irish
in the twelfth century. This was after the golden
age of saints and scholars, the Book of Kells and
Clonmacnoise. What went wrong, and why was
he saying such awful things about us?

In fact the Irish weren't especially barbaric, just out of touch. They held on to the old pagan ways after the Church had finally romanised the rest of Europe. The clergy, like their congregations, were Christian on the surface but pagan at heart. The Celtic custom was that the learned professions – bard, judge and so on – were hereditary. The professional skills were passed down from father to son. So it was for clerics: priests married, had children and set their sons up in the family business.

From an early stage, Saint Patrick seems to have accepted married clergy. One of the very first Irish Church documents is a list of decrees issued by a synod of bishops which he chaired around 457. One decree denounces any cleric who goes about without a tunic and who 'does not cover the shame and nakedness of his body, and whose hair is not shorn after the Roman custom, and whose wife goes about with her head unveiled.'

The bishops were concerned that monks and nuns should not become too familiar with each other. One decree warned monks that, if they were travelling from one place to another and encountered a nun, they were not to stay in the same inn nor travel in the same carriage as her. In fact, a monk should not even carry on a prolonged conversation with a nun.

They denounced Christians who committed adultery or swore before a druid, and threatened to excommunicate any woman who remarried according to the Brehon divorce laws. But the Brehon customs infiltrated the Church from root to branch.

Even worse, from Rome's perspective, the real power lay not with the bishops but with wealthy monasteries. Whereas on the Continent the monasteries were run by religious orders, in Ireland they were controlled by the important families and clans.

Reformers made valiant but doomed efforts to change the system. One directive allowed the clergy to marry but tried to make their marriages as miserable as possible. It stipulated that the clergy and ancillary professions should marry only a virgin, if widowed should never remarry, and in any case should abstain from sex during Lent, Advent and the forty days following Pentecost, and also on four days of every week – on every

Saturday and Sunday, and on two weekdays.

Then there was the vexed question of what went on inside monasteries. Saint Columbanus forbade monks to wash alone if naked. Not only were they obliged to hop into a communal bath, they had to sit down so that the water covered their entire bodies. If a monk lifted a knee or arm out of the water when this was not strictly necessary for washing, he was penalised for flaunting himself. His punishment was that he was not allowed to wash again for another week.

But the founding fathers had more serious sins on their minds, for which they prescribed savage punishments. So seriously were penances taken that abbots drew up lists, known as penitentials, the better to standardise them.

Here are some punishments specified for clerics by Cummean, the Bishop of Clonfert, in the seventh century. A monk guilty of drunkenness was forced to live on bread and water for forty days. If, through gluttony, he ate so much that he vomited, he was put on bread and water for seven days. If the glutton vomited the Host, he was put on bread and water for forty days. If he vomited the Host into the fire, he had to sing a hundred psalms. If a dog ate the vomit containing the Host, the culprit was put on penance for a hundred days.

A cleric who 'sinned with a beast' had to do a year's penance, while 'he who defiles his mother shall do penance for three years, with perpetual exile.' Saint Columbanus laid down a double punishment for a priest who got a woman pregnant: seven years in exile, and a diet of bread and water. If a furtive cleric managed to carry on an affair without either siring a child or the general public finding out, the punishment was five years on bread and water for a monk, seven for a priest and twelve for a bishop. A cleric who 'committed fornication in the sodomite fashion, that is, has sinned by effeminate intercourse with a male' had to do penance for ten years, living on bread and water for the first three; for the remaining seven years he was not allowed wine or meat.

Columbanus specifies a penalty of three years on bread and water, followed by a further three years without wine or meat, for the crime of 'destroying someone by magic art'. Also banned was 'using magic to excite love'. Under this category came creating abortions: the penalty for a priest guilty of that sin was three years on bread and water. Columbanus also designed penances for lay people. The penance for child abuse was a year on bread and water, followed by two without wine and meat. His penitential makes no reference to clerics committing this sin.

A Catholic can, of course, sin by merely thinking about committing a sin. A cleric confessing to nurturing carnal thoughts got seven days. If he had thought seriously about fornicating but was prevented from doing so only by practical considerations, a year's penance was his reward.

Even sex within the confines of marriage was dubious. Saint Finnian, writing in the sixth century, preached that marriage was 'for the generation of children, not for the lustful concupiscence of the flesh.' (In October 1980, Pope John Paul II took a similar view, declaring that 'adultery in your heart is committed not only when you look with concupiscence at a woman who is not your wife, but also if you look in the same manner at your wife.')

How influential were thinkers like Finnian?

It seems that they intended their rules and regulations to apply to monasteries and the tenant farmers who depended on them. If they had any idea of enforcing this regime on the community at large, it was no more than wishful thinking.

In the 1970s, an archaeology student excavated bones from a medieval monastic graveyard and sent them for medical analysis. It turned out that a form of venereal disease that showed up on the bones of the spine had killed the monks. That is probably how the good intentions of the reformers were buried.

So far as we can tell, the old Celtic religions held out no hope of an afterlife. The Irish let Christianity fill this gap, without allowing it interfere unduly with their comfort or customs. The Vatican was revolted, and gave the English invasion of Ireland in 1166 its full backing.

3

AFTER THE ENGLISH CAME

Sex. That's why the English invaded Ireland. More specifically, it was the insatiable lust of the high king of the day, Ruaidhrí Ó Conchobair, that led to the downfall of the Gael. According to the Annals of Connaught, the Pope, in despair, promised Ruaidhrí no less than six wives and the throne of Ireland for himself and his descendents if he would only stop his adulterous ways. But even six wives were not enough for the goatish king, so he spurned the Pope's generous offer. God duly punished not only the Ó Conchobair clan but the rest of the Irish too.

The more usual explanation for the Norman invasion is that Dermot MacMurrough invited them in. But MacMurrough was not only a traitor but also a sex criminal. He raped the

Abbess of Kildare and abducted Dearbhfhorgaill, consort of King Tiernan O'Rourke.

Soon after the Normans invaded, Pope Alexander wrote to the Irish bishops:

> our dearest son in Christ, Henry, noble king of the English, prompted by God, has with his assembled forces subjected to his rule that barbarous and uncivilised people ignorant of the divine ...and we are overjoyed.

As the Middle Ages dragged on, other Irish nobles followed in the randy footsteps of Ruaidhrí Ó Conchobair. Pilib Mag Uidhir, Lord of Fermanagh, had twenty sons by eight women, while Toirdhealbhach Ó Domhnaill, lord of Tír Conaill, had eighteen sons by ten different partners.

The end result of the Norman invasion was two separate communities – Anglo-Norman and Irish – each operating separate laws in Ireland. It was not until 1563 that the Catholic Church insisted that a priest should be present at a wedding; the Brehon Laws remained in force in the Irish sectors well up to then. In the Norman areas, the Church had more power. It demanded – and got – the right to try all matrimonial cases in ecclesiastical courts.

In Dublin in the late 1400s a man called Patrick Goldsmith was found to be living adulterously with a woman named Belle Bonny. The mayor backed up the stern views of the Church by expelling Belle from the city for a year. Nonetheless, Patrick sneaked out of the city and into her lodgings at night.

Speaking out against adultery could be a dangerous business. Shortly before Christmas 1585, the Protestant Bishop of Ossary, Nicholas Walsh, who was noted for his holiness and love of the Irish language, was murdered in his house by one James Dullard, whom he had indicted for adultery.

Youghal was the scene of another famous medieval crime of passion. A wine merchant called John Don lived there in 1307. He had to be away on business often, and his wife started an affair with a man called Stephen O'Regan. Don found out about the affair and warned O'Regan off, but the lovers carried on. So one night Don and some armed men ambushed O'Regan and castrated him. O'Regan sued, and was awarded twenty pounds in damages – a lot of money in those days.

Now and then, Gaelic nobles graced the Church courts. In 1451, Muircheartach Ruadh Ó Néill was up before the ecclesiastical court at Armagh for allegedly abandoning his lawful wife, Margaret Ní Mhathghamhna, for a new woman, Rose White. Muircheartach's defence was both technical and sensational. He cited a Church ban on marriages between people with 'ties of affinity.' The term denoted close relatives of anybody with whom one had previously had sex. Muircheartach claimed he had slept with Margaret's first cousin Maeve before his marriage. Therefore the marriage was invalid and should be annulled, leaving him free to live with Rose.

He produced as witness a fifty-year-old woman called Áine. She testified that Maghnus had been captured as a young man and apparently held as some sort of hostage by Maeve's father. During his captivity, Maghnus had often had Maeve in bed with him, unbeknown to her father. The witness claimed that she had shared the same bed with them, had seen them naked together and was certain they had had sexual intercourse. The case went on for two years before the court found against Muircheartach and ordered him to return to Margaret.

Other aristocrats had exuberant sex lives. When the first Earl of Clanrickard died, he left two grieving women, each claiming to be his lawful widow and her son the rightful heir. One of them was married to another man, but she had that marriage promptly annulled. Then she won the case. The second earl, Ricard Sassanach, did his parents proud, marrying and divorcing five wives in succession before ending his days with a sixth.

The Irish aristocracy produced some strong women, too. Dearbhfhorgaill O'Conor settled a dispute by leading an army against the churches of Drumcliff, where her forces 'plundered many of the clergy'. Dubhchabhlaigh Mór, daughter of the King of Connaught, Cathal O'Conor, preferred to make love rather than war. She acquired the nickname 'Haven of Three Enemies' because she married three lords who were sworn enemies of each other – and she had other men as well.

The clergy lived life to the full. The reformers made some progress after the Norman invasion but celibacy bit the dust when the Vatican started to sell papal dispensations – exemptions from Church law – to raise cash for the religious wars in Europe.

Under Church law, the children of a priest were illegitimate, even if the priest married their mother. A dispensation would legitimise them at the stroke of a pen. You sent off your application, enclosing a fee, and the stigma would be lifted. You might even get your father's job when he retired. Once again, Ireland had a hereditary clergy.

John O'Grady, Archbishop of Cashel from 1332 to 1345, had a son, also called John, who became Archbishop of Tuam in 1365. And he had a son who, in turn, became Bishop of Elphin. The O'Gradys remained in the clerical profession but, after that three-in-a-row, never got a bishop's hat again.

Another important clerical dynasty was the Maguire clan. Canon Cathal Óg Maguire was blessed with twelve daughters, one of whom married the Bishop of Kilmore, Thomas Mac-

Brady. When Cathal Óg died in 1489, the Annals of Ulster called him 'a gem of purity and a turtle dove of chastity'.

It would be no harm to put these priests in some international perspective. Pope Paul III had three sons and a daughter, dating from his days as a cardinal, by the time he got the top job. As pope, he made his grandsons cardinals when they were only boys.

But the most colourful of the Irish clerics was Miler McGrath. He started life as a Franciscan friar, then became a priest, and was consecrated Bishop of Down by the Pope himself in 1565. Miler was only forty-three then; on the face of it, he was on a very fast career track. There was just one drawback, however: this was the height of the Protestant Reformation, and Catholic clerics had a very short life expectancy in Ireland. Other Catholics languished and died in the Tower of London, but Miler – described as the most handsome man in Ireland – charmed Queen Elizabeth I, it seems. He jettisoned Roman Catholicism and was appointed Protestant Archbishop of Cashel.

He had financial control over three other

bishoprics as well. He married, had nine children and devoted the rest of his life to robbing his dioceses blind. He lived to be nearly a hundred, by which time he had virtually eradicated the Protestant faith in all the territories under his control. In 1604, the cathedral was described as 'no better than a hog-stye', and a visiting party of officials could find only one churchgoer in Cashel. Adding insult to injury, Miler made a deathbed conversion back to Rome.

There is no space here for a fuller account of Miler's corruption. Among the milder complaints against him was that he was a common drunkard and carouser, a whoremonger with a concubine in England – he would have been seventy-one at the time – and an open perjurer at loggerheads with his wife.

4

THE MORAL POLICE

You would imagine that those who had survived the horrors of the Famine deserved a break. But no – it was then that Catholic guilt spread across the land, bringing with it a virulent, spiteful puritanism.

Before the Famine, the Irish Catholic Church was easygoing. Priests went around in civvies. People still believed in *piseog*s. Drinking, courting and fighting were common at wakes and pilgrimages. In the countryside, only one in four attended church, while the figure for the cities was between one in two and three in four. Ireland had as much a folk church as an organised religion.

The bishops wanted more discipline – and the authorities backed them. The Catholic university at Maynooth received a huge annual grant from the British government. 'Is not a large standing

army and a great constabulary more expensive
than the moral police force with which the
priesthood of Ireland can be thriftily and effi-
caciously supplied?' one Westminster politician
said. A 'moral police force' is certainly what the
clergy became. Writing in 1904, the Jesuit Father
Michael Phelan looked back in nostalgia:

> Fifty years ago the priests of Ireland
> often had recourse to rough methods
> with the people. Even the aid of the
> blackthorn stick was occasionally invoked
> as an effective method of securing con-
> viction. Yet, on the morrow, all was
> forgotten and the people would die for
> the man who had punished them.
>
> Let the priest of today but thwart the
> grandchildren of that generation, even in
> a small matter, and mark the rancour . . .
> The spirit that Catholic Ireland had fifty
> years ago is sadly changed today.

The blackthorn stick was the least of the clergy's
weapons. They had a significant advantage over
the secular constabulary, who could do no more

than hang you: the clergy could add eternal damnation to a death sentence.

Nothing from Hollywood has matched the terror the Catholic Church could inspire with its searing descriptions of what awaited the sinner in hell. The sermons of the Redemptorists were proverbial. The faithful left their churches so scared that some even gave up the drink – temporarily, at least.

Guilt was an ever-present, dark foreboding. Catholics prayed for a happy death. Indeed, a number of organisations were set up for that purpose and advertised in the weekly newspaper the *Irish Catholic*. They included the Association of Our Lady of a Happy Death, which offered members a devotional outfit, including literature, a Crucifix and a Sacred Heart badge. An advertisement from 1928 reads:

> Join the Pious Clients of St Joseph's Death – the Holy Crusade for the Dying – and on the day of your death over a hundred priests will say Mass for you and millions of members will pray and offer

up Holy Communion to obtain for you
the grace of a happy death.

But it would be unfair to blame the clergy
exclusively. The new puritanism was inspired by
money and property as well as religion. In rural
Ireland, a farmer's son had to wait for decades
before coming into property. Only then could
he marry. Any accidents before then could have
a devastating effect on inheritance, so celibacy
was essential. For others, marriage was eco-
nomically prohibitive. Unless some farms were
passed on whole, they would be too small to
support anyone: this was hard luck for younger
brothers and sisters. The rise of the 'match',
with its emphasis on the dowry, also hampered
women's chances. The Irish developed a harsh
type of birth control – later and fewer marriages,
and emigration. Religion was a consolation and
a justification for this status quo.

In the 1920s, independence was followed by
the triumphalist era of the Catholic Church,
whose strictures reached baroque heights. Con-
sider the annual Lenten Pastoral Letters, written
by the bishops for priests to read out at Mass.

In a sample of eight pastorals delivered in 1923, drunkenness was condemned four times. 'Bad literature' came second, with three denunciations, followed by the evils of dancing (two lambastings). Betting trailed, with only one bishop having a go at it.

But as the twenties roared on, the bishops got stuck into sex. In 1924, the Most Reverend Dr Byrne, Bishop of Dublin, was saddened by 'suggestive dancing' and found it difficult to understand 'the feverish rush for pleasure which seems to absorb minds and energies of so many at the present day.'

Cardinal Logue pulled no punches: 'The dress, or rather the want of dress, of women at the present day is a crying scandal.' His Eminence threatened to refuse Communion to women presenting themselves 'in an unbecoming dress'. He continued: 'I have no objection to dancing as such, provided the dancing be clean, like most of our old Irish dances.' In 1925, Bishop O'Doherty of Galway advised parents to keep their daughters in: 'If your girls do not obey you, lay the lash upon their backs. That was the good old system, and that should be the system today.'

By 1928, the moral crusade was firing on all cylinders. Dancing was denounced in four of eight pastorals; drink, pornography ('vile and sensual writings, often, in their grossness, unfit even for the eyes of decent pagans') and immodest dress each merited only one denunciation. Two bishops wrote letters attacking *all* forms of pleasure-seeking.

Dancing exercised Hierarchical minds, if not bodies. The 1929 pastoral from the Bishop of Achonry explains that the clergy have to act 'because in these degenerate days vice stalks even more brazenly and unblushingly . . . One needs not a lively imagination to realise the possibilities arising from the promiscuous mingling of the sexes under conditions favourable for the machinations of wily corrupters who swoop down on their innocent prey with the greedy rapacity of harpies. Of the fruits of these midnight orgies you may learn a good deal by a visit to some of the county homes.'

These campaigns bore fruit. In 1935, the government made importing and selling contraceptives illegal, and introduced restrictions on dance halls. Dancers also faced an unofficial moral police force. The novelist Brian Moore was born in Belfast in 1921 but spent holidays in Donegal, and was surprised at how much more sex there was in the countryside than in the city:

> People went off up a lane, and you knew what they were up to. You didn't see that in the city. Boys and girls would go to dances and disappear out of the dance hall. There was a terrible lot of beating up of people – "Leave my daughter alone!"

The clerical crackdown changed the picture utterly. John Kavanagh, a writer in the *Bell*, a noted literary journal, recalled that, in his village during the late 1920s, there was a choice of four or five kitchen dances every Sunday night within a two-mile radius. A new parish priest arrived in the village in 1931, and was not content with condemning all forms of dancing:

> Boys and girls should not be on the road after dark. The CC [curate] was sent out to patrol the roads and anybody found or seen on the roads had to give their names.

Such vigilance continued for at least another twenty years. Kavanagh described a country dance in 1947:

> On the right just inside the door was a civic guard in uniform. On the left was the CC. Along the wall on the left side was a row of girls sitting up straight with their hands crossed on their knees. There wasn't even a genuine smile on any of them . . .
>
> I took a chance and picked what I thought was a fairly lively partner. As far as dancing went, we got on all right, but I couldn't even get her to smile. I might as well be dancing with the broom. Most of the dancers went round the hall one way and that meant she was facing the PP going one way and facing the CC going the other, so I tried going across the middle. It actually worked. When she found that she couldn't be seen from the stage or the door she began to laugh and chat, just as if she was at a real dance. I heard afterwards that if a girl appeared

to enjoy herself at any of these dances she could be accused of having taken drink.

In Dublin, a Father Crosbie was known for going up laneways and beating courting couples with a stick, and there were many more like him.

The moral watchdogs were easily offended. In the late 1920s a bizarre organisation was formed to campaign for women to dress in a less revealing fashion. The National Modest Dress and Deportment Crusade claimed to have 2,000 members in 1928, rising to an alleged 10,000 the following year. It had the support of at least two bishops: the Most Reverend Dr Gilmartin of Tuam gave it his 'most cordial blessing'. He explained:

> We do not want to make you all monks and nuns ... all we want is that you would restrain yourselves from sinful excess, and not allow yourselves to become slaves to pagan fashions and sinful pleasures.

How was 'immodest' dress to be defined? An exchange of letters in the *Irish Catholic* in

February 1929 gives some insight into this question. A reader addressed the Crusade:

> I would like to put before the Crusaders that they are leaving out a most important item – that is, the condemnation of flesh-coloured stockings, which are anything but modest. If the skirt was worn to halfway between the ankle and the knees with dark stockings, our young Irish maidens and mothers would get the respect due from the male sex ... Even here in this small country town, it would make any Christian's blood boil to see young girls, too – yes, even daily communicants – approaching the altar of God with skirts and stockings showing anything but modesty. I see with my own eyes young girls with skirts two inches above their knees ... Again, I notice some of these 'young ladies' cannot even in the house of God act becomingly – they sit with crossed legs, making the shortness of their skirts scandalously noticeable – and yet they venture to call themselves Children of Mary!

The registrar of the Crusade replied, explaining that a ban on flesh-coloured stockings had been in their rules at first, but since dark stockings were not readily available in provincial towns, and were more expensive than flesh-coloured ones, the Crusade had waived that requirement.

At least one very eminent man shared the Crusade's concerns. Alfred O'Rahilly, for years the president of University College Cork and one of the most prominent Irish Catholic intellectuals, wouldn't tolerate flesh-coloured stockings on his campus. He was known to examine the legs of female undergraduates to ensure that their limbs were honestly bare.

Sex education was non-existent: people learned about sex by trial and error. Some women expected the baby to be cut out of their stomachs or emerge through the navel. But neither ignorance nor repression was enough to eliminate fornication. Unmarried, pregnant girls were sent away for their term, placed in institutions to expiate their sin by washing, cooking and other hard work.

The Magdalen Home in High Park, Dublin, run by the Sisters of Charity, was the biggest receptacle for 'fallen women' in Ireland or the

United Kingdom. In 1928 Father P. J. Ganon SJ spoke about its clients in a noted sermon:

> I think not a few have been criminally foolish, if not worse ... too eager for attentions, flattery, fine dress, too addicted to dances, cinemas, music halls and the like ... been hurried by their own weakness and men's passions down the slippery slopes that end in the house of shame.
>
> But first of all, it is not for us to judge another's soul or assess its culpability ... Above all, what right have we to say that their foolishness – or wickedness, if you like – should be without hope of repentance, that they should be left forever in the misery of body and soul?

Father Gannon explained that the institution's strict discipline chaffed and galled

> those whose ruin sprang from a weak yielding to nature and whose career of sin has fostered and pampered every lawless desire of the heart ... And the religious

who watch over them must exercise a patience, a tact, a sympathy, yet withal a firmness that are not easy to combine.

The idea often promulgated by anti-Catholic writers – that the work of the penitents constitutes a secret and un-acknowledged source of income to the nuns themselves – is absurd. It leaves out of the account the heavy expenses incurred in providing their charges all the comforts needed to make them content.

In 1994, the nuns of High Park sold the cemetery attached to the institution to a property developer for more than £1 million. The site contained the remains of 133 'fallen' and forgotten women, many of whom had worked in the place all their lives. The first body had been buried there in 1865, the last in 1985.

A firm of undertakers was hired to dig them up. The remains were taken to Glasnevin Cemetery and cremated. Then the ashes were buried in a mass grave. The Catholic Press Office explained that the convent needed to raise funds for further development.

5

'MONTO'

Two casualties of the War of Independence were the country's writers and its brothel-keepers. The early years of the Free State saw a big clean-up in this area. Worldwide there was a moral panic: in 1923 the League of Nations held a special conference in Geneva to discuss pornography.

But Irish censorship was not simply concerned with pornography. It was also supposed to defend the state against what the Bishop of Galway termed 'practices that endanger the very existence of the race'. In simpler English, this meant birth control.

Under the 1929 Censorship Act, books are banned by a board of five people appointed by the government. These volunteers pass judgement on books sent in by customs officials or members of the public. One objector is all that is required to set the machinery of the state in motion.

Irish censorship was to become an international joke. In the 1930s, the censors banned an average of 133 books a year. This number increased slightly in the late 1940s, but in the 1950s the board lost the run of itself, banning more than 1,000 books in 1955.

The government responded by appointing known liberals to the board, and amended the law in 1967, by which time the notorious mass bannings had ended. By then, the censors had proscribed a truly catholic range of modern writers, including Daphne Du Maurier, Freud, Graham Greene, Hemingway, Proust, Jean-Paul Sartre, Mickey Spillane, Steinbeck, Dylan Thomas, H. G. Wells and Tennessee Williams.

By summer 1995, only a handful of books were being banned. Such titles included *Run Little Leather Boy*, *Kung Fu Nuns* and *Teachers' Orgy*. And by the end of the century, soft-porn magazines were available in most newsagents. *Playboy* found it worthwhile to register an Irish Internet domain name, *playboy.ie*.

In the old days, Irish writers were singled out.

Benedict Kiely could recall only three major writers who were not banned. He said that the Catholic Truth Society organised people to go through books, marking out the dirty passages for the censors' attention. A friend told Kiely about a neighbour who had a house jammed full of books, all sent to him by the CTS. 'I never knew the man could even read,' Kiely's friend said. One famous case was Kate O'Brien's *The Land of Spices*, banned for just one phrase: 'She saw Etienne and her father in the embrace of love.' (Etienne was a man.)

It would be interesting to know what the people who objected to that would have made of the following, which appeared in James Joyce's *Ulysses*: 'I'll do him, so help me fucking Christ! I'll wring the bastard fucker's bleeding blasted fucking windpipe.' Other passages in the work describe at some length the hero lusting, excreting and masturbating in public. There are many jovially blasphemous references to the Roman Catholic faith.

Amazingly, *Ulysses* was never banned in Ireland. When it first came out, it was seized and destroyed in both Britain and the US. It took more than a decade for the book to be published legally in those countries. The customs men had an exclusion order on it in Ireland up to 1932. Then the order lapsed, and the Irish censors did not lift a finger to stop it. There was a real danger that the greatest and filthiest of all Irish writers would remain unbanned in his native land, while minor talents got official recognition. Happily, the Board banned *Stephen Hero* in 1940, the year before Joyce's death.

'Monto', a tenement area to the east of what is now O'Connell Street, was one of Europe's biggest red-light districts from about 1820 to 1925. It was home to around 1,600 souls, and dozens of brothels operated around the clock there. The *Encyclopaedia Britannica* said that Dublin's prostitutes were more forward than those of Algiers. Some Dubliners can remember the prostitutes looking for business on O'Connell Street, Grafton Street and Stephen's Green. There was even a time when one side of O'Connell Street was for respectable people and the other for prostitutes and allied trades. The end of the Boer War was a bonanza for the madams, and in the early years of the state there was a saying: 'When the Senate is in session, Monto is full.'

Ulysses describes a drunken night in Monto. The madams call out for business, offering virgins, or 'maidenheads', for ten shillings, or fifty pence. 'Cheap whores' were a shilling, as was a bottle of beer in one of the area's many shebeens. The better establishments had a ten-shillings price, and one of the madams, Bella Cohen (a real person) protests: 'Here, none of your tall talk. This isn't a brothel. A ten-shilling house.'

Meanwhile, the customers looked out for pickpockets outside; many were robbed inside, too, especially if they were drunk.

Prostitution thrived because of atrocious living conditions. In 1928, 20,000 Dublin families were living in one-room tenements, according to the *Irish Catholic*. Of these, 12,000 families were living six to a room. They occupied the ruins of four-storey Georgian houses, with no water, which had to be dragged up in pails from a courtyard below. 'That, notwithstanding such sordid surroundings, the masses of the very poor people have such high moral standards is one of the blessings we ascribe to the influence of our holy religion,' said the *Irish Catholic*.

The masses had a kinder name for the whores: 'unfortunate girls'. These women were mostly up from the country and disgraced as a result of pregnancy. Some were domestics, made pregnant by the master of the house and packed off.

One prostitute recalled an unusual errand. She was told to have a bath and await her customer. He arrived with two bunches of scallions. Her mission was to chase him around the table, beating him with the scallions while he was nude. For this she got £20 — 40 times the normal rate.

One Dublin woman described the appearance of the 'unfortunate girls':

> Looking back on it, you can never say whether they were young or old because of the way they dressed. The usual thing was a big white apron and a skirt underneath it and a shawl. The white apron was clean-looking and it drew the attention.

Some men remembered the prostitutes as looking like film stars, however.

Local children often ran errands from the prostitutes. The women would let down money in cans on a string from their upstairs windows in the brothels. The children would buy cigarettes, matches or bottles of beer for them, and send the goods up the same way. They would keep the change for the pictures.

The father of one prostitute happened to be a civil servant. A priest approached him about his daughter's lifestyle. 'Well,' he told the priest, 'the girl appears to be enjoying herself, and besides, she's a source of income to me.'

Some prostitutes married, others didn't, and there were those who found religion. And then there were those who died from syphilis.

The Legion of Mary launched an anti-vice campaign that culminated in the closure of the brothels in the 1930s. The Legion's founder, Frank Duff, would walk up and down saying the Rosary outside the vice dens. He was supported by a Jesuit mission. Matters came to a head when a young prostitute died from venereal disease. Finally, police staged a midnight raid and closed the brothels down. Although only one madam was jailed, that was the end of

Monto. The Jesuits blessed the houses and put holy pictures on the doors.

But from the ashes of Monto, on the banks of the Grand Canal, a new vice trade arose. Right up to the late 1970s, volunteers from the Legion of Mary patrolled the canal in pairs at night, in an effort to save potential customers.

Since the 1980s, the vice industry has been thriving. The most profound innovation in this area has been the 'massage parlour' or 'health studio'. These establishments were advertised with increasing boldness, even insolence, in magazines such as *In Dublin*, which was eventually prosecuted and which subsequently toned down the advertising it carried.

The most famous massage parlour was the Kasbah, because it was one of the very few to be prosecuted. That was due to bad luck. A customer fell in love with one of the prostitutes and spent £12,000 on her. The money ran out, and her attentions evaporated. According to reporter David Mullins, the man retaliated by reporting the studio not only to the gardaí but also to the Revenue Commissioners (he estimated that the object of his affections pulled in £90 a day). There was a garda stake-out, complete with video cameras and a flurry of publicity, and eventually a woman was fined for brothel-keeping.

There were rumours that pictures of leading politicians had been captured by the surveillance cameras. One fellow, allegedly a member of Fianna Fáil, rejoiced in the nickname 'Fat-Arsed Slave'. His pleasure was to grovel to the women and, in turn, be treated like dirt by them. A Fine Gael member was known as 'The Schoolboy' because he loved being flayed unmercifully. Then there was the Labour man known as 'The Full Moon'.

Solicitors and other legal personages appreciated a damned good thrashing and plenty of discipline, according to the prostitutes. Clerics were unpopular, however, because they used bad language and had a very negative attitude.

None of these details were explored at the trial, and the inner workings of the Kasbah, which catered to an average of forty strange customers a day for more than eight years, remain a mystery.

6

THE SIXTIES

In the late 1950s the Bishop of Cork was able to stop a cinema owner from renting his premises to the local film society, which wanted to show *On the Waterfront*. As recently as 1958, a reporter from the *Irish Press* who was covering a speech by the Archbishop of Dublin showed his notes respectfully to Dr McQuaid. 'Is this really what I said?' said the archbishop, with a grin. Then he folded and tore the notes slowly. 'If that is what I said, then I hadn't intended saying it,' he continued. By no stretch of the imagination were Their Graces prepared for the 1960s, which were about to descend upon them like the wolf on the fold.

Television has been credited with bringing down the Berlin Wall. It certainly helped part the shamrock curtain. But the showbands can take some of the credit, too. They brought sin back into the dance halls. The music they played was arguably the least interesting thing about them. 'They lived well, drank a lot and fornicated at a great rate,' *Spotlight* editor John Coughlan remembered.

In Vincent Power's book *Send 'Em Home Sweatin'*, Eileen Reid of the Cadets said:

> The men in showbands had women chasing them. We knew about particular bands that were into 'bonking', as they say today. That's probably a nice way of putting it.

Yet most punters behaved conservatively. Some girls wouldn't dance with boys smelling of drink.

Times have certainly changed. Reid, who has observed a good cross-section of Irish youth from the stage, said that boys find it easier to get a girl to bed today, and aren't bothered by the fact that girls sleep around, just like them. In the more sexist 1960s, a man wouldn't want to marry a woman who slept with him before the wedding night.

Back then, Joe Dolan was a major sex symbol – and women still throw underwear at him. 'We haven't had the Wonderbras yet, no.

I think they're a bit expensive. Too expensive to be throwing away at the likes of me, anyway,' he joked. Asked whether so-called 'orgies' were as regular a part of the showband days as was rumoured, he commented:

> There were a few. We can't deny that happened, because it did. We were all very young then and everything was new.

Joe reckoned that stars could get propositioned ten times a night, 'and there are nights when you fall by the wayside, like any good Catholic.'

'There was no sex before television.' With that phrase, the politician Oliver J. Flanagan summed up the influence of *The Late Late Show* better than any intellectual. The Church was bound to come into conflict with RTÉ sooner or later; the first big row was more fun than anyone could have anticipated.

In February 1966, Gay Byrne held a spoof quiz on *The Late Late*, in which a husband and wife were asked questions out of earshot of each other. The idea was to see how their answers would tally. One question was, 'What colour nightie was herself wearing on the wedding night?' Neither of them could remember, and the wife eventually joked that she hadn't worn anything at all.

Then the Bishop of Clonfert's secretary phoned the *Sunday Press* with the text of a sermon blasting the show from a height. It was the front-page story the following day. Others got in on the act, including Loughrea Town Commissioners, the Mayo GAA Board and the Meath Vocational Educational Committee, who all deplored the program's assault on the nation's morals.

This episode was a mere appetiser to the main courses served up later: Gaybo demonstrating the use of condoms (but only on his finger), interviewing lesbian nuns and presiding over a panel which described the Bishop of Galway as a moron.

But not all the sex has been on-screen. One night after the show, a security guard intervened just in time to stop a man from stabbing someone outside the RTÉ building. It emerged that the assailant had been watching *The Late Late* in the pub when he had spotted his wife in the audience – with another man.

7

A BITTER PILL

In the early 1900s, an anthropologist made an incredible discovery on the Trobriand Islands. The people there had not figured out the connection between having sex and getting babies. Up to then, they believed that the spirits of their ancestors were responsible for conception.

But this is unique. Everywhere else, people were only too aware of the link, and from the earliest times they have tried to break it. As far back as 1,900 BC, the ancient Egyptians invented a type of contraceptive made from pulverised crocodile dung, among other things. Other methods of birth control throughout history included women jumping up and down and backwards after sex, to make it harder for the sperm to reach their destination, and sneezing in order to make the sperm slippery. A more recent, but equally inadvisable, Irish practice has been the use of cling film.

The French were manufacturing condoms in the last century, and in 1992 a collector paid $6,300 for a nineteenth-century French condom. In fact, condoms were in use hundreds if not thousands of years ago. But not in Ireland. Not until 1979 was it possible to avail of one without committing a crime.

The main opposition to all forms of contraception in Ireland has come from the Catholic Church. The Anglican bishops voted against contraception in 1908 and 1920 but changed their minds in 1930. That galvanised the Pope into action, with a broadside against family planning.

The Church once held that sex was almost always sinful, even within a Catholic marriage. Saint Augustine believed that every time a married couple had sex for any other reason than procreation or as a precaution against adultery, they committed a venial sin. Still, that was better than fornication, which is a mortal sin. Hence Saint Paul's dictum: 'Better to marry than to burn.' Saint Jerome wrote that he valued marriage only because it caused virgins to be born.

Old habits of thought die hard. Nothing could convince some clergymen that the whole business of sex and birth in general, and women in particular, wasn't dirty. The practice of 'churching' still went on in Dublin into the 1930s. After giving birth, a woman was felt to be impure, tainted or 'likened to a beast in the field'. To remove the stain of sex, she had to be blessed by the priest in church. Yet at the same time a woman could be ordered out of the confession box without absolution or forgiveness if she persisted in refusing her husband his 'conjugals'.

The inevitable result of these conflicting dogmas was the Irish Catholic mother of ten. Nearly a quarter of all the women who went to Dublin's Rotunda Hospital to have their baby in 1943 had already been pregnant nine times, according to Dr Michael Solomons. It wasn't as if they wanted that many babies. One child was born with the cap of a Guinness bottle stuck to its head – this had been used as a crude contraceptive.

In 1935, the government outlawed the importation or sale of contraceptives. There were other laws to ban any book, magazine or paper advocating 'unnatural' family planning. The Irish censors went one better: in 1942, they banned the book *Laws of Life* by Halliday Sutherland, which dealt with the rhythm method. This book had the imprimatur of the Cardinal Archbishop of Westminster, no less, but the censors were not taking any chances. Or possibly they didn't even read as far as the title page before deciding to ban it.

Although the censors had trapped many minnows, as we have seen they let *Ulysses*, a great big whale of a catch, through their nets. The same could be said of the laws against contraception: the pill was never banned in the Republic. This was because of a legal loophole. The pharmaceutical companies were able to argue that the pill was being prescribed as a cycle regulator, as opposed to a contraceptive. It has been available since 1963.

Dr Kevin McNamara was a staunch and loyal conservative Irish bishop. But here is what he was saying in 1967, shortly before Pope Paul VI denounced 'unnatural' contraception:

> In changed circumstances, the ban against contraception might be withdrawn. Today it could be argued that such a change exists. The problem today is overpopulation, not underpopulation. Today, too, the status of women is completely different . . . It is not now clear that the ban on contraception cannot be revoked.

Dr McNamara was merely echoing the view of clerics the world over. Between 1963 and 1966, a Papal Commission in Rome studied contraception and, although it had a strong conservative element, voted overwhelmingly for changing the Church's teaching. Clerics like Dr McNamara were preparing their flock for a dramatic change. But they were the ones to be shocked, when Paul VI issued *Humanae Vitae,* prohibiting Catholics from using any form of contraception.

Father Jim Brandes saw the newspaper headlines at breakfast after *Humanae Vitae* was published. 'The first words out of my mouth were: "Oh shit!"' he told author David Rice. Father Brandes got severe cramps that lasted for weeks but disappeared once he decided to quit the priesthood.

Could the Pope have foreseen how furious and how widespread the outcry against *Humanae Vitae* would be? Many priests rebelled. In Cork city a liberal priest was well known for reassuring Catholics in the confession box that the pill was not wrong. One day a letter appeared in the paper under his signature, denouncing contraception. No one was more surprised than the cleric, who discovered that his bishop had written it.

In the past thirty years, around 100,000 priests have left the ministry. Before leaving the priesthood, David Rice advocated the use of the pill. He felt he had no choice after hearing a woman explain that she had being saying no to her husband since the Pope's announcement, and when he didn't get sex he beat her up and did it with the dog.

In the Northern Hemisphere, *Humanae Vitae* has been rejected overwhelmingly. Like cigarette advertising, it is retreating to the developing countries. But back in 1969, when the first family-planning clinic opened in the Republic, the vast majority of the Irish population opposed contraception. Only 167 new patients visited the Irish Family Planning Association's first clinic in 1969.

Now the pill is one of the most widely prescribed drugs in most Irish medical practices.

The Republic of Ireland has since become the largest manufacturer of oral contraceptives in Europe. This is thanks to the Industrial Development Authority's success in attracting chemical and pharmaceutical companies. Several of these companies produce the pill.

The courts, not the politicians, decriminalised contraception in Ireland. The Supreme Court made the landmark decision in 1973, when it interpreted the Constitution as guaranteeing a right to privacy for married couples. Following on from this, it ruled that Mary McGee, who brought the case after customs officials had confiscated some spermicide she ordered, was entitled to import contraceptives for her personal use. A family-planning clinic broke the law if it sold contraceptives, however. A barrister found a solution: the clinics should simply give contraceptives away, while soliciting voluntary donations.

This loophole was tested when a John O'Reilly wrote to a clinic for an information booklet and some contraceptives. He also had his daughters, aged eleven and nine, sign or transcribe other letters, at his direction. These letters were posted, with money enclosed. Contraceptives were sent back, whereupon he made a formal complaint. He alleged that clinics had sold the contraceptives, and to very young girls. The Irish Family Planning Association was not to know that Mr O'Reilly was a member of the Irish Family League. He would be one of the leading lights in the pro-life campaign of the 1980s. The clinic was prosecuted, but a district justice threw the case out.

The information booklet that had been implicated in this case – a guide to family planning published by the Irish Family Planning Association – was the subject of further legal action. In 1976, the Censorship Board banned it as 'an indecent or obscene publication'. The publishers went to the High Court, which found against the censors. The Censorship Board appealed to the Supreme Court, and lost again.

There was a sudden upsurge in censorship in the late 1970s. In a four-month period, the board banned no fewer than 117 books and three magazines, including the feminist publi-cation *Spare Rib*. The conservatives were girding their loins for the pro-life battles ahead.

8

CONDOMS AND CLOWNS

Prophylactics have caused one major political crisis and several minor ones, and are responsible for the formation of a new political party – the Progressive Democrats. That condoms were illegal never meant that they could not be obtained. It was easy to order them from advertisements in British magazines. The first family-planning clinics used to get friends and family to import contraceptives in suitcases. They also found that flat, handwritten envelopes got through the post.

In 1971, the customs men got their come-uppance. A group of Irish women's rights protesters, in the heady days of bra-burning and miniskirts, went up to Belfast for contraceptives and returned by train, laden down with booty. They challenged the customs men to arrest them for a flagrant breach of the law but the authorities backed down.

The first attempts to legalise contraception were made in the early 1970s by a number of senators, including Mary Robinson, who introduced private members' bills in the Senate. Subsequently, the Supreme Court forced a change in the law when it ruled that a married couple had a constitutional right to contraception. This created the anomaly that contraceptives were acceptable under the Constitution but criminal under the law. It was obvious that the law had to be changed, but this took six years – and two governments.

The first effort ended in high farce. In 1974, a Fine Gael–Labour coalition put a bill to legalise contraception before the Dáil, only to have it voted down by rebel TDs, including the Taoiseach himself, Liam Cosgrave. Cosgrave had not given the Cabinet or the other government TDs any inkling of his intentions. They suddenly found themselves looking rather foolish. The defeat would have been even greater if Cosgrave had bothered to warn his colleagues of his intentions. It seems that some TDs only voted for the bill in the belief that he was supporting it. Cosgrave was among the last to vote, and these TDs were corralled in the 'Yes' lobby before they realised their mistake.

The second attempt, in 1979, was Charles Haughey's much-derided 'Irish solution for an Irish problem'. To be fair, this act legalised contraception. It also set out the provision that condoms could be sold only by a pharmacist in a chemist's shop to someone presenting a doctor's prescription, however. And the doctor could issue a prescription only to a married person using contraceptives for 'bona fide' family-planning purposes. The 'bona fide' clause was unenforceable, as its wily architect must have guessed.

One effect of the new law was to make condoms more expensive – a doctor's consultation fee (even with a repeat prescription) would cost far more than a packet of condoms. And then there was the chemist's dispensing fee.

But to a certain extent, what the politicians decided did not matter. As late as the mid-1980s, only a quarter of the state's chemists were prepared to stock the 'sheaths of Satan'. Bona fide or not, you were bawled out of it in their shops for asking for a packet of condoms. But there was another statistic: by that time, 30 million condoms had been dispensed by family-planning clinics.

When moral legislation was being drafted, ministers had previously called around to the bishops' palaces. During the Mother and Child row, Noel Browne was offered handmade cigarettes from Bond Street and champagne in the afternoon when he dropped in on the Bishop of Galway. Haughey consulted all the religious leaders. This time, however, the bishops had to troop in to the Customs House to see Haughey: a small step for secularisation.

Dr Andrew Rynne has at least two firsts to his credit: in 1973, he was the first doctor to perform a vasectomy in Ireland, and ten years later he was the first to be prosecuted under the new law for selling condoms. Dr Rynne supplied condoms directly to a patient one weekend when the chemist's shops were closed, and was fined £500. Later, Judge Frank Roe lifted the fine, but warned: 'Anyone without condoms at the weekend will have to wait until Monday.'

Efforts to liberalise the sale of condoms continued, and led to a political crisis in 1985. A Fine Gael–Labour coalition led by Dr Garret

Fitzgerald proposed a bill that removed the need for a doctor's prescription to obtain condoms, but allowed only over-eighteens to buy them. The joke this time was that the law would allow people to marry at sixteen but force them to wait for two years before using a condom. Condoms could still be sold only in chemist's shops or clinics.

This modest bill, introduced by Barry Desmond, got through the Dáil by the skin of its teeth. Another coalition – between Fianna Fáil and the bishops – fought it. Dessie O'Malley was the only Fianna Fáil politician to support the proposed legislation, albeit passively. He threatened to defy the party whip by abstaining rather than voting against the party. He abstained from the vote, being unavoidably detained from the Dáil when the vote was taken. He was expelled from Fianna Fáil as a result, and ten months later set up the PDs. Thus, paradoxically, the Progressive Democratic Party owes its birth to a contraceptive.

Then came the AIDS epidemic, and health authorities across the globe urged young people to use condoms. But the Irish Family Planning Association was fined £400 for selling them in Dublin's Virgin Megastore; this fine was increased to £500 on appeal. The uproar over this prompted Charlie Haughey, back in power and a born-again liberal after Mary Robinson's dramatic presidential victory, to hint at a change in the law.

The Archbishop of Dublin intervened immediately. Dr Desmond Connell 'found it extraordinary that no political party in this country is prepared to defend what so many people regard as fundamental values of family life.' But the Hierarchy could no longer stop the tide.

In the 1990s, under Albert Reynolds – a staunch conservative if ever there was one – the age limit for the purchase of condoms was finally removed, condom vending machines were allowed and restrictions on the type of outlets selling condoms were abolished. Newsagents now stock them, and the machines are found in many pubs.

Figures from the Central Statistics Office show that imports of condoms have increased almost sixfold since 1979. In 1993, the Republic imported 50,859 kilos of condoms – the weight of fifty-three Volkswagen Polos. The imported condoms were worth £898,934. British manufacturers had 97 per cent of the business, followed by the USA, Scandinavia and the Far East.

9

THE BISHOP'S GIRLFRIEND

There are seventeen orgasms in the first 200
pages of Annie Murphy's book *Forbidden Fruit*.
That works out at one every twelve pages, giving
Jackie Collins or Harold Robbins a good run for
their money. Murphy declares that the former
Bishop of Galway, Eamonn Casey, was the best
lover she ever had, before he betrayed her – and
you'll take her word for it.

Best of all is the episode in Eamonn Casey's
car one morning. The bishop was a notoriously
fast driver, and as his car was zooming through
the countryside at its usual kamikaze speed,
'without him even touching me I threw my head
back and gushed with a noisy orgasm.' His
Grace was suitably impressed.

By the time Murphy published her book, the
whole world knew the story. But the incidental

details, coupled with a great ear for the former bishop's turn of phrase, make it a fascinating read. For instance, the book gives a very thorough account of the bishop's prowess as a lover:

> He was a voyeur of his own sexuality, which he had denied himself for so long. He saw himself kiss me all over and he delighted in his own expertise. He saw himself bring me to orgasm, filming everything in his head, as it were for the years to come.

If you remember the Friar Tuck-like Casey from his TV appearances, your mind will boggle at the descriptions of him dancing naked in front of a blazing fire before making love on an Afghan rug, while Frank Sinatra sang in the background. The morning after the couple first made love, Casey had a great appetite, eating two lamb chops for breakfast. Also consumed in the course of the affair were vast quantities of booze and a fair sprinkling of tranquillisers.

The affair ended with pregnancy and pain for Annie Murphy, and returned to haunt the bishop in May 1992, when she told her story. As the news was about to break, Casey flew to Rome to resign, and then to Central America to repent. If he had held a confessional press conference or appeared on television, as do most celebrities when their personal problems are revealed, it certainly would have helped the Church handle the sensation. Instead, the affair dragged on, with the bishop moving on to South America, fleeing from one journalist and then talking to another. He made a short but disastrous visit home. He was photographed outside a church, decked out not in sackcloth and ashes but in his full episcopal finery. It looked like a picture of the Church triumphant, and outraged many Irish Catholics.

Casey was also photographed in the midst of Irish soccer fans, whooping it up at the World Cup in the USA. Annie Murphy returned to Ireland early in 1995 to appeal to the Church to let Eamonn come home again. She told journalists that Eamonn now phoned their son, Peter, and that father and son were buddies.

The scandal coincided with an abortion referendum, provoked by the 'X' case. In this case, a young girl was raped and became pregnant. On learning that she intended to go to Britain for an abortion, the state prosecuted her. The courts lifted that injunction, ruling that her life was at risk: there was a danger that she might commit suicide, the courts stated.

This inhumane prosecution shocked liberals and Catholic churchgoers alike. Abortion had always been illegal; that ban was reinforced by a constitutional clause forbidding it, following a pro-life referendum in the 1980s. Now the outcry galvanised the coalition government into a second referendum, which diluted the provisions of the first one and offered women the right to information and the right to travel abroad for abortions if their lives were at risk. The bishops appealed for compassion and understanding for Eamonn Casey and, having done so, could hardly pursue the pro-choice lobby with the spite displayed during the first abortion referendum. And there was worse to come.

In November 1994, a sixty-seven-year-old priest collapsed and died in a gay sauna club called Incognito in Dublin. He was dressed only in a towel. Two other priests were on the

premises and gave him the last rites. A spokes-
man for the club said, 'We have lots of priests
as members. In fact, priests are next after
barristers and solicitors in our membership.'

Parishioners turned on the media. 'You are
all bullshitters. Why don't you go away? Tell the
people that Gerry Adams has the government
round his little finger and is running things,' a
local man advised a *Star* reporter. The government had recently legalised homosexuality; at
least the reverend father didn't die a criminal.

Rumours about priests spread like wildfire.
Father Michael Cleary was hugely popular for
his radio chat show and other show-business
activities but detested by liberals for his stridently
expressed conservative views. Eighteen months
after Cleary's death, his housekeeper, Phyllis
Hamilton, told the *Sunday World* that Father
Michael and she had been living together for
twenty-seven years as man and wife. They had
had two children, one of whom was adopted.
Hamilton's mother had threatened to approach
the Pope on him, but had been won around in
the end, Hamilton said.

The day the *Sunday World* article went to

print, Cardinal Cathal Daly reiterated that there would be no surrender on celibacy. The controversy raged on, fuelled by the Church's admission that another priest, Father Pat Fenlon, had had a child with a local married woman. Father Fenlon went on leave while the *Sunday World* and the *Star* pursued the news. When he returned to his Portlaoise parish, he got a standing ovation at Mass. There was also a darker scandal: paedophile priests.

The most infamous clerical child abuser was the late Father Brendan Smyth. In 1994, a UTV television documentary revealed that Smyth had been molesting youngsters for decades. The Church's response over the years was simply to move him from diocese to diocese – a cover-up that widened his trail of misery.

Twice the Catholic Church arranged transfers for Smyth to America, and twice he offended there. Eventually families complained to the Church authorities in Northern Ireland, who tried to persuade them not to 'go public'. When the Church took no action, the families went to the police. Smyth was charged and questioned by the RUC in Northern Ireland in 1991, received bail and promptly skipped to the Republic – which was, of course, a separate jurisdiction.

For three years he sheltered in an abbey in County Cavan. Extradition warrants were served against him, but there was a mysterious delay in processing them. (The fact that extradition warrants issued in April 1993 were never acted upon led directly to the fall of the Irish government in November 1994.)

Father Smyth was extradited to the North in January 1994 on nine charges, nearly four years after the police investigation had begun. In June he pleaded guilty to seventeen charges dating from the 1960s. After serving a term in the North, he was rearrested and jailed in the South for offences committed there. He died in prison and was secretly buried at night in the Norbertines' Cavan monastery.

Taoiseach Albert Reynolds lost office at the height of the controversy. With hindsight, it is clear that, in the panic of the moment, he was unjustly vilified for his part in the matter. Not so the Catholic hierarchy. The revelations of a concerted cover-up, wilful self-interest and disregard for both the laws of the land and the safety of children in its charge have shaken its moral standing irreparably.

The Smyth affair encouraged many other victims to come forward. Now, whenever a priest or brother is jailed for child abuse, the news barely makes the front pages. The Church has issued qualified apologies, paid compensation, and issued some justifications. Its moves were seen as late and begrudging. In 1994, the *Sunday Tribune* reported that, when a priest knocked on a door in Dublin during a parish visitation, the young man who answered said, 'Sorry, Father, there are no children in this house,' and slammed the door.

The Church may be down, but it is not out. It has lost the battles on censorship, contraception, divorce and homosexuality. The pro-life debate rages, however, with another abortion referendum to further the pro-life cause looming on the Irish political horizon.

Whatever the outcome of such a referendum, one thing is certain: irrespective of the law or the Constitution, people will use every possible means to keep doing what humans have been doing for as long as our species has been on this earth.

SELECT BIBLIOGRAPHY

Adams, M. *Censorship: The Irish Experience.* Dublin, 1968.

Carlson, J. *Banned in Ireland.* London, 1990.

Kearns, K. C. *Dublin Tenement Life: An Oral History.* Dublin, 1980.

Kelly, F. *A Guide to Early Irish Law.* Dublin, 1995.

Lee, J. *Ireland 1912–1985.* Cambridge, 1989.

Moore, C. *Betrayal of Trust.* Dublin, 1995.

Mullins, D. *Ladies of the Kasbah.* London, 1995.

Nicholls, K. *Gaelic and Gaelicised Ireland in the Middle Ages.* Dublin, 1972.

Ó Corráin, D. *Ireland before the Normans.* Dublin, 1972.

Power, P. C. *Sex and Marriage in Ancient Ireland.* Dublin and Cork, 1976.

Power, Vincent. *Send 'Em Home Sweatin': The Showband Story.* Dublin, 2000.

Solomons, M. *Pro-Life? The Irish Question.* Dublin, 1992.

Watt, J. *The Church in Medieval Ireland.* Dublin, 1972.